FOOTSTEPS

Perspectives for Daily Life

Rebbetzin Esther Jungreis

SINAI LIVE BOOKS

Imprint of Rethink Partners, Publishing

Rethink Partners books may be purchased for educational, business or sales promotional use. For more information please contact Rethink Partners, LLC at info@rethinkpartners.com.

ISBN-13: 978-1469984674
ISBN-10: 1469984679

In celebration of Hineni's 40th Anniversary
A gift of love to you

The Torah teaches us that 40 is a special number for a blessed new life. We offer you just a few thoughts on this magical number 40:

The flood of Noah lasted 40 days, after which he emerged from the ark to create a new world – a new life.

Moses ascended Mount Sinai, stayed for 40 days and brought down the Torah.

The Jewish people wandered in the desert for 40 years and then went forth to the Promised land.

At one time or another, each of us finds ourselves lost in a desert.

This little book is presented to you with a prayer that G-d lead you out of your desert, guide you to your promised land and enable you to build a blessed new life.

As we of Hineni celebrate our 40th anniversary, we invite you to join us so that together we may create a new, committed Jewish life for all our brethren, wherever they are.

With Blessings and Love,
Rebbetzin Esther Jungreis and your Hineni Family

לזכר נשמת חיה פייגל גולדה בת יצחק

For the sponsor of this book:

In loving memory of her mother
Chaya Feigel Bat Yitzchok

Rebbetzin Esther Jungreis is a Holocaust survivor who has devoted her life to inspiring people to reach for their fullest potential. In 1973, she founded Hineni, an international center for learning and spiritual reconnection. Learn more at Hineni.org.

Introduction

"Don't waste the opportunity, the gift that G-d gave you, that is your life."

As you may know, I am a survivor of Bergen-Belsen. Prior to our deportation, we visited my grandparents. It was a bitter winter. I was sitting on my grandfather's knees and I found him weeping. I didn't know why he wept. My father explained it to me – he took a walk with me on the snow and made a path for me. And he told me that my grandfather was making that path for me when he was learning and praying. Every one of us had a grandfather someplace that made a path for us, who wept for us, who prayed for us.

My grandfather was killed in Auschwitz, but he lives! Because his footsteps are here. And the footsteps of your grandfathers are here. We just have to follow them.

Journey

Life is one big journey. Sometimes the ride is very bumpy. And sometimes you get a flat. And sometimes you fall into a pothole. It doesn't mean that you have to stay there forever. You don't. You get out of it. The main thing is that you should not live "Iftory". What is "Iftory"? People say "If this wouldn't have happened, if that wouldn't have happened, if I wouldn't have made that wrong decision, if this, if that, if that."

Iftory doesn't work. It is history. What happened — happened. In Hebrew we say, "What was, was." What was — was! It happened. It is over. Move on. Move on. Get going! Don't obsess over the past. It is three "w's": don't wallow in the past, don't worry about the future, but work today. I remember meeting once a lady who said to me, "Rebbetzin darling, if I had only met you thirty years ago, how different my life would have been." And I said to her, "My dear friend, if only I had met me thirty years ago!" Because thirty years ago I didn't know the things I know today. But you have to move every day. You have to become stronger and wiser from yesterday and not wallow in the past. It is not Iftory. Get going today!

We have a teaching from King Solomon, "Seven times a righteous person falls and stands up." What do you mean seven times a righteous person falls and stands up? In order to become righteous, you fall. But then, you stand up!

Purpose

Everyone has a unique mission in life. No one is a duplicate. We are all custom made by G-d and propelled unto this planet for a special mission—for a purpose. We all have to leave behind the calling card. We all have to know that because of us, the world was a little bit better; it became finer. We touched some people, we touched some hearts, and we made a difference. We didn't just grab and take; we made a difference in the life of others.

Don't cook for just yourself. Cook for the world. Cook for others! Invite them to your table or send food to the poor—to the indigent. If you have nothing else to give, give a smile. A smile is so precious. It is such an awesome gift to give to someone. It doesn't cost you anything but it goes so far in changing the life of that other person. And then the smile comes back to you.

Everyone has to give. Life is about giving. Discover what your unique talents are. Focus on them and give them away!

Free Will

People often ask me, "Is there really such a thing as free will? I mean, am I really in charge of my life? To what extent am I in charge of my life? If G-d is in control of the world, if there are no coincidences, and if everything comes from Him, then what am I? A puppet? Why should I be held culpable?"

There is an amazing teaching, "Everything is in the hands of G-d except your reverence for G-d." Meaning, whether you are short or tall, wise or dull, healthy or ill, is determined by the Heavens Above. You have no choice in it. You have no choice in the family you are born into. Before you were born, you didn't have an opportunity to go shopping and say, "This is the mother I want and this is the father I want." No. G-d propelled you unto this planet, placed you in the body of a woman and that is it. You had no choice on it. Some people are born into dysfunctional families; some people are born into very solid families. So is there a choice? Some people are born handicapped and some people are born brilliant. Is there a choice? Not in that.

But there is a choice—in that which really makes a difference. It does not matter whether you were born this way or that way. It does not matter which family you were born into. The only thing that matters, that counts, is your belief in G-d.

But how does belief in G-d grant you free will?*

As I explained, it is not in our hands to choose the family into which we are born, or our DNA. But what is in our hands is our reaction to that which is our lot in life... whether we choose to be angry – bitter, kind or compassionate, generous or selfish. At the end of the day, that is the only thing that counts. So whether we are physicians or plumbers, whether we are in academia or business, whether we are impoverished or wealthy, has no relevance in the Heavens above, but how we handled that wealth, how we reacted to that poverty, is the scale on which our lives will be measured. And that will depend upon our belief in G-d, who charged us with a mission to love our neighbors as we love ourselves.

At the end of the day, it is that which will sum up our lives and that is the meaning of free will.

Confidence

Nervousness is normal. There are moments where if you were not nervous, it would be abnormal. Everything that G-d gave us is positive—if you want to make it positive. So if you are nervous, ask yourself, "Why am I nervous?"

When we want something to be good, we prepare ourselves. So it is good that you are nervous because otherwise you wouldn't be prepared. You wouldn't take time to dress properly; you wouldn't take time to organize your thoughts. So if you are nervous, organize yourself and think, "What am I going to say? What am I going to wear? What am I going to do?"

Then you have to know that one little prayer will help you along the way. And that is to say to G-d, "O Mighty G-d, please walk with me. Please be with me. Help me. Show me. Guide me. And You give me the words."

As you know, I never speak from a text. I always speak from my heart. Before I speak there is one little prayer that I always say to myself. It is from King David's Book of Psalms: "O G-d, open my lips. And allow my lips to praise Your Holy Name." Because we need G-d's help to guide and guard our tongues. We need Him to help us organize our thoughts so that we should be able to speak properly, say the right words, transmit the right feelings, and communicate the proper emotions and energies. Nervousness is good—prepare yourself and talk to Him, that He should help you and He will!

Misfortune

Bad things do not happen to good people. It is just that we do not understand it. So let's try to dissect this subject a little bit.

First of all, ninety-nine percent of the bad things we encounter in life are self-inflicted. We create our own problems—and then we accuse G-d! Why did you do this to me?! But we neglect ourselves; we abuse ourselves. It is written in the Torah, "Behold, I give you a blessing and a curse. A blessing if you are going to follow my commandments, a curse if you are going to abuse and ignore my commandments. If you are going to ignore the commandments, there are consequences." Similarly, if you don't take your medication, there are consequences. You can't scream, "Look what happened to me!" If you ignore the doctor's instructions, there are consequences. That is one factor.

In the book of Psalms, Psalm 23, it says, "Your rod and your staff shall comfort me." Sometimes G-d has to give us a little bit of a push, a little bit of a slap to wake us up, to make us realize, "Hey! You are doing the wrong thing." When bad things happen, instead of saying, "Why? Why? Why?" we should say, "What do I learn from this? How can

I improve myself? What is the message that G-d is sending me?" Because G-d is always sending us messages. It says in the book of Deuteronomy, "You shall know in your heart that when a father punishes his children, that is how G-d punishes you." When a father punishes his children, does he really want to punish them? No. It hurts the father more than the child! But the father is inflicting that discipline so the child should mature and come to his self-realization.

Loneliness

Loneliness is actually the most painful experience that a person can have. If you want to punish someone in the most severe way, put them in solitary confinement. There is no one to talk to. You are alone. And yet, amazingly, we find that when the Almighty G-d created man, He created him to be a lonely being—why? Animals were created two by two, male and female did He create them. Adam was all alone. Only later on did G-d create Eve—why? Because man had to yearn for a partner. He had to understand, "I need a partner, I cannot be alone." And to everything that is negative, there is also a positive side.

So when you are alone, you have to look within yourself. You have to become creative. Adam had to search his soul and had to come to the conclusion that, "I need a partner. I need someone to share with." And that's how man attains a level where he can give, where he can share. But in order for him to appreciate the sharing that he is giving, first he has to experience loneliness.

Joy

It is not easy to be happy. It is easier to be moody. It is easier to be sad. It is wonderful to be happy but you have to work very hard to be happy.

The word for happiness in Hebrew is "Simcha." It is made up of two words: "Sheh mochel" meaning "to erase." You have to know how to erase the bad things from your mind. That is not easy because we have a tendency to obsess over problems. It is like a broken record that keeps going in our minds. We have a bad experience and it just keeps going in our minds.

Jealousy is also very sad because it deprives you of happiness and joy. If you are jealous, you can't enjoy what you have. You are always thinking about what the other guy has—and it bothers you! Here you have a nice little apartment, you have everything that you need, but because somebody else has something more, you can't enjoy it. So happiness is something that is really hard to come by—you have to work on it. Part of that is freeing yourself of jealousy and bad thoughts. Just wipe it out! My husband, Rabbi Jungreis, of blessed memory, used to say, "Bad thoughts? Pshh, wipe it out! Just like that!" And you know, if you think about it, it helps.

An excellent tip to find happiness is to learn to

smile. If you put a smile on your lips, it will go into your heart. As a matter of fact, I was speaking on a college campus one day, and a student came over to me and said, "Rebbetzin, can I ask you a personal question?" I said, "Sure sweetie, what would you like to ask?" And she said, "I read your books; I know you went through so much. How is it that you are always smiling? Can you tell me, where does your smile start, on your lips or in your heart?" And I said, "Let me think about that. I never thought about it."

And then I told her, "My smile always starts on my lips because in my heart, of course I have worries, of course I have fears, who doesn't? But you know, you have a responsibility to others that your face is public property. You don't want to take away other people's good moods because of your grouchy and long face. Such a face can spoil the atmosphere—it spoils parties, family dinners, family gatherings, and so forth. When someone comes in with a moody face they just spoil it. So you put a smile on your face, and from your lips it goes into your heart. And from your heart, it goes to other hearts and back to your heart. And you learn to be happy!"

The Soul

The soul is not something that anyone can examine. It is not something that you could see. But every morning, in our prayers we say, "The soul that You gave me, O G-d, is pure. You have created it. You have breathed it into me."

You could mess up your mind, your heart, and your deeds, but you could never mess up your soul. Because it is the part of G-d in every human being. Every human being is a part of G-d. G-d breathed into us—the breath of G-d is your soul. It is pure. The soul hurts when a man sins. The soul and the body are in constant conflict. The soul wants to do good. The soul cannot abide evil—it recoils from evil. The soul cannot tolerate injustice.

But the body is very demanding. So very often, most often, the body overcomes the soul. And the soul is crushed. Most people's souls in our society are anorexic. They are terribly, terribly neglected. They are suffering from undernourishment. These souls are suffering because they receive no vitamins, no energy, and no nourishment.

What is the nourishment of the soul? Spiritual activities. What is spiritual activity? What is spirituality? The soul only can be spun through that which is spiritual. What is spiritual? Is it meditating? Is it sitting in a yoga position? Is it climbing the Himalayas? Is it being a vegetarian? No, because all those things are self-centered, self-focused activities. There is nothing spiritual about them. In Hebrew, the word for spirituality is "ruach." Ruach comes from the word "wind". Do you see the wind? No. But what do you do with the wind? You feel it! The wind can only be felt.

A spiritual man, a spiritual woman, is someone whose love is felt. One who is able to reach out to others and others are able to feel that person. When you are able to convey your love to others and make a difference in their world, you are a spiritual person. By sitting in a yoga position, by having a vegetarian diet, by climbing the Himalayas, or by meditating, you are not touching anyone. It is not the wind. You don't see the wind, but you feel the wind. A spiritual person is someone who you feel.

The soul is nurtured on spirituality. The soul is nurtured on the word of G-d, "Not by bread alone does man live." Before we eat we make a blessing and through the blessing we extract the spirituality from the food. We connect with G-d through everything and that nourishes the soul. When you sit down to study Torah, your soul is nourished. When you pray, your soul is nourished. When you reach out to others, your soul is nourished.

The soul is always pure. The soul is that little voice that makes you feel guilty when you do something wrong. The soul is that little voice that wakes you up in the middle of the night and whispers to you, "Don't do that, start a new life." The soul gives you pain. So you run to the therapist, you take a pill, you take a drink, you are upset. But that is just a Band-Aid. The pill, the drink, the therapist do not take away the anguish of the soul. Because the soul is pure. And the soul is demanding that you live a pure life.

Self Worth

Self-esteem is something that is natural, that should be natural. It should be automatic to every person—if he realizes who he is. It is unfortunate that children are not taught who they are. You stood at Sinai. G-d spoke to you. You are a part of the Almighty G-d. You are part of the Almighty G-d! I mean, can there be a greater incentive than that? You are holy! Because G-d's holy spirit is in you!

You have a mission—to fulfill the task that G-d assigned to you. Every person was created custom-made by G-d. There are no two people on this planet earth who are exactly like you or exactly like me. We are all custom made by the Almighty. You have a unique task, a unique purpose. It is tragic when children are raised without understanding this, because they become very unhappy adults. They can even become self destructive, becoming addicted to drugs or to alcohol. They can have all sorts of problems in their marriages and in their relationships. Because they do not understand that they have a purpose—that life has meaning. So it all goes back to one word: "Torah, Torah, Torah."

Wants versus Needs

Happiness, our Sages teach us, is to be found in being content with what you have. In our world, in our culture, people do not take pleasure in what they have but they agonize over what they do not have. So can you imagine how happy you would be if you would take joy in the possessions that you already possess, instead of looking to see what the other guy has and you don't have. That is our own doing because we have been born into a culture that is constantly teaching us to want more because we need more. You don't need all those things. You'll never be satisfied. Because the more you have, the more you will want. So take pleasure in what you already have. Not in what you want to have.

Balance

It doesn't matter whether you are a cab driver or a physician. The question becomes, what sort of a physician do you become? Or what sort of a cab driver do you become? If you are a cab driver who is kind, generous, sweet, and good then you make a difference in the world. If you are a physician who is miserable, tyrannical, and arrogant, you destroy people!

It is not what you have in your pocket but what you have in your heart! That is what counts. And that will depend on your reverence for G-d. Because if you believe in G-d, then you'll be different. There are some people that have millions of dollars and they are miserable. There are some people who have just a few dollars and they change the world. It is what you do with your life. That is where you have your free choice. So instead of becoming bitter and angry about what you don't have, capitalize on what you do have and improve the world.

Money

Money is something that in our world we think is the G-d. People worship money. For money, people kill. For money, people will destroy families. I can never get over that! Sometimes families come speak to me — spouses are not talking to each other, mothers are suing their sons, and sons are suing their mothers. It is incredible! Over what? Over money! Money is the root of all evil. You cannot take it with you. When you die, you die with empty hands. The only thing you can take with you are your good deeds.

Restraint

Discipline. Discipline. Discipline. That's our Jewish, Torah way. The whole Torah is one big discipline. "Sanctify yourself with that which is permitted" means you should be disciplined even with things that are permissible. You are permitted to eat—but don't make a pig of yourself. You are permitted to drink wine—but with a limit.

In the Torah, we find that discipline is one of the principles of our lives. You have to be in control. If you are in control, then you are able to live your life with meaning and happiness. It is written, "Who is strong? One who can control his desires." That is a strong man.

Ask a person, "Who is a strong man?" and they'll say, "Somebody who has a strong body, such as a bodybuilder" or "Someone that is powerful financially." No. The strong man is he who is in control of his desires. Who is able to say, "That is it. Enough." One who is able to withstand temptation—and that is not easy. Because we are constantly being seduced by so many voices. So many messages!

Control. Control. Our entire Torah is control. From the moment the child is born we teach them about control. For example, we cannot mix milk and meat. You had meat? You can't have milk now, sweetie—you have to wait. You want to eat something? You can't eat it without first you having to make a blessing. You have to wash your hands for bread. Today is Shabbos, you can't turn on the TV. It is not "I want!" It is not having a temper tantrum. It is not instant gratification, which is such a sad disease in our generation. It is not "I want it now!" Discipline. Discipline. Discipline. It is not venting and telling people whatever you feel like saying. It is about control. Control your tongue. Control your appetite. Control your greed. Control your passions. Sanctify yourself in that which is permissible.

Creativity

It is natural for man to be creative because G-d created us to be creative. Each person has a unique mission to create. You have to discover what that mission is and what you should create. So you have to be a perceiver, believe in yourself, have dreams, have a vision, and you have to try and try again. But first and foremost is prayer. That ultimately leads to knowing who you really are—knowing your talents.

It is important to know your faults. It is a tragedy if you have too many faults but if you know them, you perhaps can rectify them. But you know what is the greatest of tragedies? Not to know your assets! Not to know your own ability! Not to recognize that which you can create. And we all have that ability—to create something and to make the world a little bit better. G-d gave us life. G-d created each and every person custom-made. We are not the production of a mass company. We are not mass production. G-d created each and every individual with special love. Each and every person is unique—there is no other individual in this world that looks exactly like me or exactly like you. Similarly, there is no other person in the world who has exactly the same neshama, the same soul.

One day, when you have come to the Heavens above, G-d will ask you, "Did you fulfill your creative mission?" The great Rabbi Zeesha would very often say, "On the Day of Judgment, I'm not going to be afraid if G-d says to me 'Why weren't you like Abraham, David, Isaac, or Jacob?' I will simply say, 'O Mighty G-d, I never had those gifts. I couldn't create like they created. How could I aspire to become Abraham, David, Isaac, Jacob, Moses, or Jeremiah? How could I do that?' So I won't be afraid. But if G-d says to me, 'Zeesha, why weren't you like Zeesha? Why didn't you fulfill your own creative ability? Those gifts that I gave you—why didn't you use them to your best potential? Why didn't you make the world better with the creative ability that I gave you?'"

Goals

You remain young as long as you can dream. Dreams are important. You always have to have a vision. You always have to have something to look forward to and something to aim for—you have to have a goal. I may be dreaming but I'm not sleeping.

Jewish Identity

We are a nation that sealed a covenant with G-d at Mount Sinai. We have a unique relationship with Him—to be His witnesses, here on planet Earth. There can be no greater privilege than that. In the book of Isaiah it is written, "I created this nation so that they might sing my praise." Why are we Jewish? To sing the praise of G-d! Can there be a more awesome challenge than that? There is no one in this world who is exactly like you. There is no one in this world who is exactly like me. But who are you? Discover it! You owe it to yourself! It is a tragedy to live your life without knowing who you are. It is the greatest privilege to be a Jew. It is the greatest catastrophe to not be aware of that privilege.

About the Author

Rebbetzin Esther Jungreis was born in Hungary and experienced the Holocaust firsthand as an inmate of Bergen Belsen. Following the war, the Rebbetzin devote her life to combating the spiritual holocaust that we are witnessing here in the United States and around the world.

Hineni

In 1973, Rebbetzin Jungreis founded Hineni, an international movement to inspire the Jewish people to return to their roots. Hineni programs have been held throughout the United States as well as in Israel, South Africa and Australia.

In 1982, the Hineni Heritage Center opened its doors at 232 West End Avenue in New York City. Today, the Center offers a comprehensive series of programs and classes on the Torah, Talmud, Kabbalah, History, Rituals, Hebrew language, and much more. There is a constant flow of visitors through its welcoming doors, and visitors leave fortified with a knowledge of their roots, and with the desire to learn more.

Visit Hineni at www.hineni.org or contact the organization at hineni@hineni.org.

Books and Columns

For more than forty years, Rebbetzin Jungreis has written a weekly column for The Jewish Press using the Torah as the source for solutions to everyday problems. In addition, thousands tune in for the Rebbetzin's Life Transforming Weekly Torah Class, which is live-streamed around the globe.

The Rebbetzin Jungreis' books include:

Jewish Soul on Fire
William Morrow & Company, 1982. Named one of the ten best Jewish books of the year by B'nai B'rith.

The Committed Life: Principles of Good Living from Our Timeless Past
Harper Collins, 1999. Now in its eighth edition and translated into multiple languages.

The Committed Marriage
Harper Collins, 2004

Life is a Test
Mesorah Publications, 2006

Torah for Your Table
Mesorah Publications, 2009

Speaking and Recognition

Rebbetzin Jungreis has been acclaimed by the Jewish community throughout the world, and her outstanding work has been recognized by Hadassah, The Jewish War Veterans, B'nai Brith, Federation of Jewish Women's Organizations, Knights of Pythias, and the Christian Amita Society. She has been the keynote speaker at the joint convention of Reform and Conservative Rabbis in Palm Springs, and has spoken for the Rabbinical Council of America, O.R.T., Hadassah, U.J.A., B'nai Brith, and many more. She has also been accorded recognition by the State of Israel and invited to address members of the Israel Defense Forces. Her seminars attract overflow crowds.

Note: Biographical information courtesy of Hineni and The Harry Walker Agency

About Sinai Live Books

 Sinai Live is committed to assisting high-quality teachers share their wisdom. Our goal is to enhance our readers' personal Jewish journeys and elevate everyday life through thoughtful and insightful content. We aim to engage, inspire and encourage further exploration.

Our books include:

 Telushkinisms: Wisdom to the Point by Rabbi Joseph Telushkin

 *Insights: Concise and Thoughtful Jewish Wisdom* by Rabbi Benjamin Blech

 *Passport to Kabbalah: A Journey of Inner Transformation* by Rabbi DovBer Pinson

Visit www.sinailive.com or contact us at info@sinailive.com to learn more.

About Rethink Partners

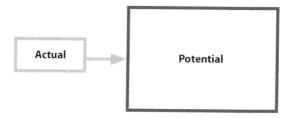

This reading experience was developed by Mark Pearlman's Rethink Partners, an organization dedicated to shifting user and industry perspectives through a combination of business strategy, product management, sales and marketing, editorial, design and online implementation.

Rethink Partners works with for-profit and non-profit organizations to help them reach their potential. We are focused on seeing both what is and what could be.

Visit us at www.rethinkpartners.com.

Acknowledgements

This book would not have been possible without the help of many people. Special thanks goes to:

Barbara Janov, for her tireless efforts in managing Hineni and making it all happen. She is the behind-the-scenes person every successful organization needs to be exceptional.

Mark Pearlman, for documenting the Rebbetzin's teachings on video over the past decade, for helping hundreds of thousands of people access her lectures and teachings via the Internet, and for his initiative to create and publish this unique book.

Jake Laub, for his creativity in design and diligence in editing.

Raquel Amram, for her meticulous transcriptions and editing.

Jon Winer, for his expertise in video editing and production.

4318941R00023

Made in the USA
San Bernardino, CA
10 September 2013